Winnower

Winnower

Poems

AARON BROWN

RESOURCE *Publications* · Eugene, Oregon

WINNOWER
Poems

Resource Publications
An Imprint of Wipf and Stock Publishers
199 W. 8th Ave., Suite 3
Eugene, OR 97401

www.wipfandstock.com

ISBN 13: 978-1-62564-486-2

Manufactured in the U.S.A.

for Minda

CONTENTS

ACKNOWLEDGMENTS

I would like to thank the following literary journals for publishing these poems:

Illya's Honey: "Africa to Europe"
Kodon: "Sea Burial" and "Taxi #442" which appeared as "Yassin"
North Central Review: "Automaton Man (A Life)"
The Pub: "On the Chadian Civil War"
Warscapes: "Memory Across Ocean"
Windhover: "Evacuation Ebenezer"

My thanks also to Minda Brown, Eric Kozlik, and Will Fargason for revision help.

INVOCATION

The woman bent to gather grain onto the woven straw,
piled the millet in the center, then elevated the shallow basket,

hovering it five feet above a cracked ground. Her parched hands
quivered to support before she let gravity draw the seed down,

down to a pan of purity. In the wind, the chaff wandered as I did along
the rutted road when I first saw her, the woman on the plain

with no hut or tent in sight. I longed to join her in sifting
memories, watching the refuse of bullets, lies, loss melt away—

to glean the ripeness of belonging: the steaming *shai*, the afternoons
conversing with friends of a past life, hard to distinguish in the haze

that swirled around her, enveloped her till she and all my visions disappeared.
If I will find her again, I must wander this road through a land

not fully mine but more of me than anywhere else.

I

MEMORY ACROSS OCEAN

I have been shielded from the suffering
of earth's most silent heroes:

the aged woman
stooping low to boil her tea,
on a crude black grill underneath a tree;

a man pushing himself through sand
with his gnarled hands,
crippled legs folded in between—
his trail stretches for miles behind;

or the smoldering homes of lives
scattered like some shrapnel—
once released there is no returning.

The smoke rises from the capital
and its citizens mill about with whatever
memories of the old life in hand;
taking their chances past the police checkpoints,
braving the overflowing bridge to another country.

In another country, I sit with a pen.
Somewhere across oceans of water,
oceans of sand where my life began
I had everything to dispose of,
though my people had nothing.
They watched their country
in one day rise up in smoke,
in flames that I could board
a plane to escape, listen to the engine
hum my soul away to where
contemplation is the only means
of return.

SARIHAT, SOUTH OF THE DUNES

The herd of camels encircles our village. The beasts shift silently on their feet with the moon giving birth to their shadows. We sleep across a mat laid out on the sand-grass. One man mumbles something, another ventures out into the dark to relieve himself. Still, others remain awake to muse about the spirits that follow you at night, spirits you turn to never see.

Finally, the dawn dew seeps into every fiber of my clothes, every dead blade in the grass mat, and I am bathed into wakefulness. I lie still as the men perform ablutions, washing with vigor their feet and arms and hands. They join together to pray toward the sunrise, to the bustling Mecca in another world. One of the nomads walks to the nearest camel and empties her of milk, bringing the full bowl to us. We each draw from it and pass it on.

DURING KHARRIF

We held the mangos in our hands,
the skin ripe and firm, and sliced
until we had a plateful of gold.

We puffed out our bellies as if pregnant
and laughed, talking politics and soccer
over glasses of mango juice.

Outside, rainy season winds skittered
twigs and *hadjlij* seeds across the earth,
a thickened cloud hovered like soot

over the horizon, threatening to spill its
entrails upon the leaves outside my door.
The yard would erode, the bricks disintegrate

in a wash of sand and rain—a deluge
that could not drown the whir of the blender,
the scoop of spoons in the sugar jar.

BROKENTREE

Where all who wanted rest would come,
the once-mighty *haraza* tree lies shattered.
By the shores of the dry river,
it rose to a lofty height
to block out the sun—
twisting, waving, sighing.

But now it lies broken.
People come to see its ruins,
thinking of how it must have been
before they raise the axe and descend,
ravaging the wood for their fires
before day's end.

ONE SQUARE MILE

These, the bullet holes in my friend's wall, when during rebellion
a man ran into the yard chased by soldiers who fired upon him.

They found his comrades hiding on the back porch—
bound and lined them in the dirt, shooting one by one.

This, the street where a tank demolished a wall to position
its nozzle in view of all who journeyed down to death's door.

Then, the checkpoint where Dawoud was pulled off his motorcycle,
held at gunpoint. *We have killed so many today, so why not you?*

There, the Libyan Hotel where peacekeepers stay in five-star luxury.
The hotel where I wandered in with two friends, rode the elevator

to the top and back and sipped coffee, asking how so much
could take place within a few hundred yards.

ON THE CHADIAN CIVIL WAR

I

West of Abéché

How he must tremble now
in a ripped-up uniform,
Ahmed, the boy who smiled.

He told our town he was visiting
family in the east—really
he was lying, wanting to see

the might of those washed-out rebels,
to find truth in the legends sung
of those card-playing bandits.

The news came to us
a few hundred miles away,
rumors underneath the *nim* trees.

Watching the government trucks
rush to border battlefields,
we sipped our tea, shuffled

cards for another game of *basara,*
talked of Ahmed who visited family
in the east.

II

East of Abéché

Some meet death in shredded uniforms,
while others still hold Kalashnikovs,
shaking in their boots

as they try to distinguish
friend from foe in the night.
Fast-taken steps on sand—

shouts of anguish, of command
flood the desert like a rainstorm
on a tin roof, the thunder rattling

above, all around. A helicopter
swoops down above a truck,
its driver shot, haphazardly

weaving between the short bushes:
those shrubs that will burn your skin
if you touch them.

FOLLOWER

Followed by a demon, the soldier tried to think from where had he been trailed.
The speakeasy? The gendarmerie? The market where he had picked up a pack
of cigarettes without leaving a coin?

He forced the thought from his mind, focused on the headlights coming down
the tree-lined street, the way the beams seemed a two-eyed moon cloud.

But always the steps behind him coming: across the soccer field and chipped-
paint parade grounds, through the street between the empty granaries
and the lean-tos awaiting camel-selling nomads.

The tin door to his house was crooked, the lock he fumbled with,
and the yard empty, waiting. Lowering his head, he passed underneath
the doorbeam of his one-room hut where his woman turned in her sleep,
exhaled, and so did he with breath that stank of fermentation.

The demon was out in the yard, but he could not walk out to meet it.

Then, the soldier's daughter stirred, rose for a midnight drink from the clay jug
underneath the acacia, leaving her mat and leaving the hut and going out
into the night, silhouette against the sky.

He wanted to warn her, to raise his arm to shield her, but his mouth was dry,
eyes unfocused. He tried to close them but could not. Sweat stained
the uniform he wanted to take off but could not.

The metal tin covering the jug rattled. It rattled no more.
His daughter was in the clutches of the follower.
He must go out to meet it.

The soldier saw it, silent and small—huddled in the middle of the yard.
He took aim and fired.

BULLET

Brass-capped bullet
heated to molten flow,
I wonder how you
vacated the chamber
and what you struck to stop.

The metalworker
fashions you anew,
melting bullet to cast
a bronze statue—
triumphant swordsman
atop rearing horse.

But you will always be the bullet—
fired on some remote plain
to silence the voice of a rebel
stirred to speak, now resting
undisturbed.

EVACUATION EBENEZER

I

This is my altar
built with the rubble of memory:
trembling walls, echoing gunfire,
rotors beating the air above.
Hither by thy help I've come.

We tested the silent street when
the submachine gun emptied its clip.
Shutting the gate, we rushed back
to our cream-colored chapel, our house,
which we consecrated then in prayer.
Have mercy, Lord, for the sounds
of my enemies are all around.

We gathered in the living room,
placing mattresses over the windows,
crouching behind the chairs and couches.
Knowing only to whisper your name.

II

Christus Victor,
you broke into my house
when the gunshot sounded
and looters scaled the wall.
I watched shadows pass outside the windows.

Sandals scuffed the hallway,
our bodies huddled quivering,
and the metal grate twisted with the crowbar.

Then gathered in the back room,
we listened to the dull beat of their voices
indistinguishable, intoxicated.

Naked I came, naked shall I return.

A looter in warm-up pants entered—
with his wide eyes he seemed
surprised to find us staring back at him.
But still he raised his hand and shook:
Cellphones. Money. Jewelry.

The shadow reached out, grabbed what he could,
disappeared to join the others—
his young face mirrored my own.

III

The quiet house was littered
with what little of life
we chose to take.

The emptied shelves, opened bags
strewn across the floor, dust
floating underneath
the pale fluorescent light.
And after the fire, a still small voice.

Outside, the dull bullet-echoes ceased.
The wind came like a gentle whisper
across the sand grains on the pavement,
like a breath through the embroidered drapes,
swelling and suspended.

BACKFIRE

I have returned. Footprints in a thick layer of dust. Suitcases with airplane tags in a pile in the corner. I lie in my bed and listen to the street sounds with the lights outside shining through the shutters, webbing shadows over my face. Crickets tick away the hours from underneath my bed. Outside, two men are talking, but I only hear sounds and not words. A motorcycle takes minutes to whir by and minutes more to fade into the night.

A bang from the street, and I am awake, my heart beating faster. But I can no longer think of emptied gun clips. I must sleep even when a car backfires.

II

WE HAVE COME TO AMERICA

These night-drives, when the electric
    skyline watches over us,
these memories I absorb because I am with you,
    my brother, mother, father.

Rhythmic streetlights lull us
    to silence in Dallas,
where the saturated air murmurs
    lotus petal belief.

Where every concrete café and mannequin
    display insulate us from the truth
that materialism blindfolds
    these night drives.

We no longer have the desert,
    with gentle windswept
nights lit by stars—
    now streetlamps hum highways.

Our memories are hard
    to catch in fingers delving
the well of thought.
    We must draw deeper from the old life.

AFRICA TO EUROPE

I spent the day wandering Montparnasse. Parisians filtered out of streetside shops and cafés as if through revolving doors, and I was among them, but for what reason I could not tell. I entered department stores with pristine products on display—just watching, not buying. Euro price tags fibrillated my heart because I was from someplace where you can buy what you want for change, and though it may not last, it fulfills its purpose and does it well.

I entered a church, cool silence and vaulted ceiling. Old women stopped by from their afternoon strolls and lifted prayers up to the stones. I entered a park where immigrant men played *bocce* and where the kids smiled and pointed to the apartment complex, *La grande maison du ghetto*. And when I was finished, I turned at the bakery onto my street where the small door opened into a courtyard of trees that seemed transplanted just like me.

MERSEYSIDE

I sit on the wharf
watching the tide encroach
upon the exposed bar, the sun
setting behind the smoke stacks of
a cruise ship and factories.

I had gone to the Anglican Cathedral—
despite what people say modernity
draws from the old, here recreating
the sublime in a sea of brick houses.

The Cathedral tower is moored in
maroon stones planted on a hill
over the Liverpool quarry, now
St. James's Garden, where stones
of a different nature mark out death
and dialogue with the leaves
a dialogue of peace.

But in this garden a group of men laugh,
tipping heads back to expose bad teeth, scratching
shaved heads as they shift in fading football jackets.
Elsewhere in the garden, young intellectuals
drink liquor out of soda bottles, talk in hushed tones.

The tombstones and trees can no longer converse—
the sloshing and laughing are too loud. Modernity
encroaches not as a resurrected Victorian effort
to build a house of God, but as a silent protest
in the shadow of the church, the closed church
bolted after five o'clock, where an entry fee
is charged during visiting hours while outside
an Irishman with a scabbed face pushes his child
in a stroller and begs for change, an American
demands weed, girls paint their faces to attract,
and cacophonous songs blare from an outside concert—
notes off-key, sound waves echoing off museum walls.

And still I hear the gulls crying
over the police sirens, the bus brakes,
the fireworks celebrating the weekend.
The sea gulls make the crying sounds
of a dying breed.

PRIMUM MOBILE

We are two souls drawn together
in an airplane conversation,
flying Chicago to Dallas,
talking of Islamabad, Istanbul,
N'Djamena, Nairobi, Abu Dhabi.
In all these, the diversity in culture;
the importing and exporting of race;
how tribal thinking holds nations back;
religion, mysticism married to orthodoxy;
corruption, the vice that suffocates the people.

He is a communication man,
the type who's travelled around
to make sure that everyone talks,
that everyone pays their bills,
while my family saw the world because
something, someone told us to help.

What moves us? He asks.
What motivates?

Try as I might I couldn't say,
God.

CHICAGO MOSAIC

This is my cathedral where I worship:
where the thousand fleeting shadows pass
down one gridded street to the next
from State to Michigan to Oblivion—
souls busied out of reality.

We enlist for the great assembly line:
detailed, mechanical, cemented
into waking up for the early commute
and bedding down to the television sounds.

Yet I must confess that I am not from here,
though I act like I am.
I am from a thousand different places,
but now call here, home.

I've learned to join with the others
to dream of feet walking in unison,
treading out time like distance runners
clocking in for the human race.

The towers rise, the streets fill
with people walking faster now—
a testament to the light in the distance
where these man-made towers stop

in awe of the unconquerable expanse,
that is the world outside our own.

TAXI #442

His operator's license reads, "Yassin Said."
Born in Yemen, now working in Chicago,
Yassin makes his living
driving half-drunk Americans
from one bar to the next.

He remembers the drive up from Sana—
the hills and roads that dangle you
on life's edge, and the soldiers who
stop your car and search for weapons
and rebels.

He remembers how you can buy an AK
for the same price as a fare from Lincoln Park
to the Water Tower.

And he remembers
the sand-walled streets
where boys play football
and old men sip hot water
soaked in the husks of coffee beans
exported to America.

Now he drives two routes downtown.
He buys cups of Yemeni coffee
and smells the steam rising
from the rock-soil
of his country.

SEA BURIAL
on the death of Bin Laden

While many shout in the streets
and wave starred and striped flags,
there is a ceremony at sea
with your bullet-riddled corpse.

They wash your stained body,
wrapping you in a pure cloth
until you lie pristine and prepared,
serenaded by an empty eulogy.

The plank is lifted and you cast off
in a fluttering plunge, your mummified
corpse sinking into the only thing
that will receive you.

To a cloud of foam
and the dark, quiet depths
your half-blown face goes.
It hides in the black.

Perhaps along a faraway shore,
a boy skips stones and sees a white-
wrapped body on the waves,
coming towards shore.

HYMN

I cannot come to this city
to use it, taking the train in then out.
I must give it full attention,
as in the arms of a lover,
wandering aimlessly

   underneath the fluorescent tiles,
those blinking windows which
   mosaic each tower; beneath the marquee
bulbs flashing "Chicago" down on State Street,
   gilding upturned faces; through the throng
of nine-to-five plodders marching
   to the train that will take them home.

I focus on these faces, these motley Midwesterners
and transplants like me. I focus on the rickety
looping train, the pixilated water-spitters, and
the pan-handlers, masters of wit.

I venture down each line and let it lead,
finding Chicago in its glamour and in its grim.
Steel red-brick gray-stoned bastion
   of stories.

THE ARAB IN THE CORNER OF THE CAFÉ

The Arab man sat beneath the television,
his eyes fixed on me squirming,
writhing like a cat caught in a child's arms.

I don't know what he thought as he watched
with steady gaze, with doleful eyes,
with an understanding that comes from crossing continents.

Am I me, or am I someone else trying to be something else
in a place in town where all the tangents meet?
Tell me, his eyes seemed to say. *Tell me, or you will be exposed.*

APPARITION

My wife hadn't seen him, the man who seemed an apparition,
the man with the cane lurching along the curb as if maimed
by war or by a market bus. He was dressed as the men in Chad
dressed with a white *tagiye* on his head, a shirt of gossamer cotton,

but the shirt caught for him the drop-heavy summer air coming
in on Atlantic winds rather than Saharan ones, droplets suspended
in place of granules. He knew the asphalt sidewalk like he knew
the mud and rut of another world when one greets neighbors

and asks about the harvest, but instead we were driving in rundown
Maryland, driving with our headlights illuminating leafless trees
full of plastic bags and plastic bottles, illuminating this man walking
beside a pond full of rusted bikes, slick-oil ducks, cast-off garbage.

He must have been swept in on a desert wind, a sand-grain vision
sent to me in my time of night, to never forget the dust I am from
and the dust to which I return.

ELEGY
for Madri Abdel-Aziz

The feeling when
the list of people I know
grows smaller; when

I hear the words
on the phone, in a text
—"I have hard news for you"—

when all I have left and
all I can do is mourn
the way you repeated

the name of my girlfriend,
"*Melinda,* she must be beautiful,"
when I told you of her;

the way you stood like
warped timbers supporting
the thatched *lugdabe*

giving shade, offering rest
to drunks, wife-beaters, lost souls;
the way you never knew your father,

executed outside the city limits,
and how your newborn daughter
will grow with only a week-old memory.

Mourning, my heart is in mourning
for the loss of another,
too soon and too deep,

the loss of a father to his newborn,
of a husband gentle and caring.
I mourn the loss of a brother

in smile, in jest, in faith.
I see a thousand shadows of you a day,
in the street or underneath a tree,

and I know that while your bones
lie buried in the earth, your spirit
ascends in a paradox of existence.

Heaven has become a necessity,
necessary to exist for all whom I have lost—
a place to reunite and sip *shai* underneath the *nim* trees;

to play poorly-played soccer and talk of the distance
between our lands as if nothing; to put to death
the question of whether I will ever see you again.

AUTOMATON MAN (A LIFE)

That night, I wept for you.
How I've opened then shrunk
at the hammer and anvil clanging
(more often of my own doing than yours)
—not feeling worthy, like a surprised friend
realizing all the guests gathered
are gathered for him.

I wept for childhood.
The drawn-out videos of turbaned singers
ensconced in carpeted television studios,
an outside boy in an outside world
all too foreign yet familiar: a spectacle.
Spectacles taken off to the world,
unclear and unfocused, I realized the
diaspora of my friends, of me, of feeling
from Montreal to Ouagadougou.

I wept for silence.
The cool, numbing injection
of silence that follows a question.
They also serve who only stand and
what went wrong with my world?

I wept for God.
The oil to my creaking gears,
to my aluminum limbs rising
before the splitting curtain.

That night I wept for all—
all who have come to see
this "Amazing, Unfeeling,
Automaton Man."
(Show starts at 7pm).

www.ingramcontent.com/pod-product-compliance
Lightning Source LLC
Chambersburg PA
CBHW051049030426
42339CB00006B/276